ASSESSING CREDIBILITY

INTERNAL MISCONDUCT RESPONSE TRAINING

MARCUS WILLIAMS

WILLIAMS & CO. PUBLISHING

TABLE OF CONTENTS

About the Author

Marcus Williams began his investigative career as a private investigator.

Marcus became a police officer with the Pentagon Force Protection Agency in 2001 in Arlington, VA and protected Pentagon employees, rescuers, and investigators after the terrorist attack of Sep 11, 2001.

Marcus joined the Naval Criminal Investigative Service (NCIS) in 2002 as a Special Agent criminal investigator. He became an expert in family and sexual violence investigations and operations, to include sexual assault, sextortion, child pornography, domestic violence and Internet based crimes. Marcus was a squad leader and Supervisory Special Agent. He led efforts involving local, state, federal, international, and military jurisdictions.

In 2017, Marcus became the Deputy Title IX Coordinator for Students as the primary investigator of sexual misconduct at Brigham Young University. He was instrumental in building policies, procedures, and processes for the Title IX Office.

Marcus served with NCIS in Twentynine Palms, CA; Sigonella, Sicily; Norfolk, VA; Everett, WA; Yokosuka, Japan; and San Diego, CA. He currently provides misconduct training, coaching, and support to business, education, and government clients.

Marcus Williams graduated from Brigham Young University with a BA in International Politics and minor in Latin American Studies. He earned an MA in Criminal Justice from American Military University.

Introduction

Assessing Credibility - A Complex, Yet Straightforward Skill

Investigations involve human beings, and every human has unique experiences, beliefs, education, background, culture, and values. All of these factors drive their perspective and motivation. You may try to extricate the human element from your investigations, but that is an impossible strategy. A fraud investigation may require months of detailed examination of financial records, with you stuck in a room stacked with overflowing file boxes. A network intrusion investigation may require that you stare at a computer screen for hours on end dissecting lines of code. But ultimately, every case leads back to a human being; and human beings are multi-faceted and complex.

Ultimately, it is your job to put the puzzle together piece by piece to determine what actually happened. You will find it necessary to assess the credibility of every person involved in the investigation. You are reading this book to develop those skills.

Here are the topics we will discuss in this book:

1. Importance and relevance of credibility

2. Standard of Evidence

3. How to assess credibility—evidence-based practices

4. What weight should your assessment carry?

5. Pitfalls and limitations on credibility assessments

In this book, we won't address interviewing skills or techniques. That's a subject for another book, or better yet, an entire training program. The more training you receive in proper interview techniques, the more adept you will become at asking the right questions and gathering the best information. We also will not discuss bias in investigations, although we will touch on the role of bias in a credibility assessment. We will discuss how statements obtained through interviews combine with gathered evidence to create your credibility assessment.

SECTION 1

WHO NEEDS CREDIBILITY ASSESSMENT SKILLS?

Everyone conducts dozens of credibility assessments a day. You subconsciously assess every person you come in contact with and allow that assessment to guide your interaction. All of your decisions are guided by credibility. Even if you never meet the person, you will assess his or her credibility through the email they wrote, the website they host, or the tone of their phone conversation. Unfortunately, most of us do a poor job at assessing credibility. We allow biases and preconceived opinions to influence our thinking.

Whether you applied for a position as an investigator, or you have been as- signed to do investigations as a part of your job, it is incumbent upon you to develop your skills. You *cannot* allow subconscious assessments to guide your investigations. You must be cognizant of what you are thinking and why at every step in the investigatory process. Ultimately, you must be able to articulate in writing why and how you came to your conclusion.

Even if you are not an investigator, developing the ability to make deliberate and accurate evidence-based credibility assessments will help both your professional and personal relationships.

Section 2

What Is a Credibility Assessment Anyway?

Whenever you interact with another person, you make a decision on whether or not they are telling the truth; in essence, you decide that they are either spreading "fake news" or speaking truthfully. This tendency is born out on social media every day. Competing views will post information regarding the exact same incident. Often one perspective paints a very positive picture, while another perspective presents a very negative one. I am not referring to disagreement over the subjective interpretation of facts, but rather the issue of relaying the objective details of the incident in an altogether different way. How do you decide which one to believe?

You will often approach an interaction with a preconceived opinion and then wait to see if the other person confirms your opinion. You may allow your biases to unjustly dictate your assessment, only considering evidence in the way that confirms your opinion, and further disregarding or explaining away evidence which does not. This phenomenon is known widely as *confirmation bias*. Social media is a hotbed of confirmation bias.

EXERCISE 1

Take a minute now to look at your social media feed. You will find posts and articles which match your beliefs. Algorithms keep track of all of your posts, likes, and shares in order to curate your feed with the information sources most tailored to your values and beliefs. This creates a sense that the people around you all believe as you do.

If you have a friend who shares opposite views, ask to look at his or her feed. You will recognize that their feed depicts an alternate reality, where the exact same events are communicated in a completely different way. This exercise should help you realize that you do have preconceived opinions and biases. We all do. Credibility assessments require you to deliberately put those aside.

People do not generally speak in terms of absolute truth or absolute lies. Most conversations sit somewhere on the scale between the two absolutes. Think about the last time you told someone a story regarding an incident you thought was important or hilarious. Review that conversation in your mind before you continue reading.

As we review the topic of credibility, be candidly honest with yourself about how you told the story. Is it possible that as you told the story you noticed your friend's eyes glaze over and saw she was quickly losing interest? Possibly you added a detail here or an embellishment there to make the story more exciting and engaging. Maybe you embellished how close the other car actually came to your bumper when he cut you off. Maybe you described yourself telling off your boss a little more aggressively than you actually did. Maybe you included what you wanted to say to your ex, rather than what you actually did say. I am going to assume that you are not a liar. You did not begin the story with the plan to deceive your friend. Instead, you assessed her interest and adjusted your story accordingly. Afterwards, you thought nothing of it. Your friend probably suspected you had embellished details, but she didn't call you a fraud or a liar. It was an expected and accepted social interaction.

Imagine that the other person wasn't your friend, but was an investigator. Again, your intention was not to lie or mislead the investigator. You simply took a socially acceptable conversation and tried to drop it into a situation where it was no longer acceptable. You were suddenly expected to tell "the truth, the whole truth, and nothing but the truth." But ninety-five percent of your story was accurate, so what was the harm? Now imagine that the investigator decides, based on the embellished five percent, that you were not credible, and therefore elects to discount your entire statement. Suddenly, the case falls apart. If the investigator had been properly trained to make a comprehensive evidence-based credibility assessment, he would have been able to move forward with the case. You are now that investigator.

A credibility assessment is a formal process of determining whether a person and/or information is credible or believable. In an investigation, you are determining if you can and should believe one party over the other. Ultimately, you are deciding which statement will carry more weight in your conclusion.

SECTION 3

IMPORTANCE AND RELEVANCE OF CREDIBILITY

When discussing the importance and relevance of credibility in an investigation, I am reminded of the bedtime fable, *"The Boy Who Cried Wolf."* In the story, a young man reached an age where he was finally old enough to tend the town's sheep herd on his own at night. His father told him that if the herd was ever threatened or in danger, he could cry out and the townsfolk would come running to his aid.

During the first long night, however, he became lonely and bored. Out of curiosity, and in search of company, he cried, "Wolf! Wolf!" The townsfolk came running with pitchforks and torches, only to search the area and find no wolf. Angrily, they returned to bed. During the second night, the young man again longed for some excitement and so cried, "Wolf!" The townsfolk came running in their nightclothes and slippers, ready to defend the herd, but there was no wolf. On the third night, the young sheep herder heard a rustle in the grass. He peered over and saw two angry yellow eyes staring at him. He heard the low growl of a wolf and felt his stomach drop. In a panic, the young man cried out desperately, "Wolf! Wolf! Wolf!" until he was hoarse, but no one came. The young man did his best to defend the herd alone, but the next morning the townsfolk found him standing, dejected, next to the slaughtered herd.

This fable is often told to children to teach them not to "cry wolf;" the lesson being that if you are known to tell lies, no one will believe you when you tell the truth. After all, isn't it the young man's fault that the town lost their sheep? We teach our children to be honest from an early age. As a parent, I can't count the number of times "Mr. Nobody" made a mess in our house. In the popular comic strip, *The Family Circus*, creator Bil Keane even created recurring characters Ida Know, Not Me, and Nobody. He depicted them as transparent outlines of children and who the real children frequently blamed for all sorts of mischief. We also often teach our children that they will get in more trouble for lying about something than the original act itself.

But let's turn the wolf story on its head and think about it from another perspective. Who really suffered the loss in this story? All of the town's sheep were dead. The young man would have probably lost his job if there were still a job to lose. But really, he survived the night, and they weren't his sheep. He only lost his future as a sheepherder, something he clearly wasn't cut out for anyway. The townspeople were the big losers in this scenario, so why are they not the focus of the story? For our purposes, we will focus on and learn from the townsfolk.

Although the young man did make two false accusations against the wolf, the third accusation was true. The wolf feasted upon the herd while the townsfolk plugged their ears and snuggled deeper under their covers. The townsfolk decided that he was no longer credible after the first two nights, and ended up losing their entire herd because of it. They collectively made a credibility assessment and used that to dictate their response on the third night. Unfortunately for them, two false reports did not make the third report false as well. The result of their presumption was the loss of a valuable asset.

Each report should have been handled independently, even if to do so seemed a nuisance. What could they have done differently? Here is a list of potential solutions:

1. Assign a second trusted herder to keep the young man company.

2. Assign one person to respond if he cried wolf to verify the story.

3. Discuss if the young herder was truly ready to be on his own.

4. All continue to respond to every cry.

5. Provide the young man additional training and explain the impact of his actions.

Exercise 2

Take a moment now to write down any other potential solutions you can think of. These five are by no means the only options.

This is of course a fictional account with fictional potential solutions. However, considering the tale as a real scenario is still a valuable exercise in understanding the importance of credibility assessments. Every proposed solution would have required work or effort on the part of the townsfolk. To have prevented the sheep massacre, they needed to take additional steps to either prevent or better understand the situation, so that they could have made better decisions.

By making an across-the-board credibility assessment without putting in the proper effort, they ended up losing. They became annoyed, and allowed their annoyance with the young man to dictate their own personal decisions, ultimately defaulting to the easiest option: ignorance. They blamed the massacre on the young man and taught future generations not to "cry wolf," never admitting they could have prevented the catastrophe through their own due diligence. In truth, everyone in this situation bore some fault.

Section 4

History Is Important, but May Not Be Relevant

It is important for you to assess the credibility of all parties regarding information directly pertaining to the investigation as well as other relevant and related incidents. This includes looking at their history. But wait a minute, I just castigated the townsfolk for basing their assessment on the sheepherder's history of false reports. Not exactly. The first two nights of crying wolf were relevant to their credibility assessment. But as I stated, they needed to take additional steps before they decided on their final course of action.

You should always look at the history of both parties and review their employee/student records or past incidents. There may be incidents in the employee's past that are relevant to the current investigation. Think of it in terms of a law enforcement investigation. One of the first things a detective does is run a criminal history check on a suspect. Does the history prove the current allegation? Of course not. But it can definitely show patterns, preference, *modus operandi*, etc. What if the detective is interrogating the suspect and the suspect claims, "I would never do that," yet the detective knows that the suspect was convicted of doing that very thing five years ago? The detective is laying the groundwork for a credibility assessment.

Using the same example, if a suspect is being interrogated for sexual assault and the criminal history shows an arrest for shoplifting, that probably isn't relevant when the suspects says, "I would never do that." Context and detail matter.

What if this is the third allegation of harassment against the respondent? That should open an avenue of investigation. Are there three different complainants? What are the circumstances surrounding each allegation? This history is good information, but again, not necessarily determinative. Every bit of information is another piece of the puzzle. It is your job as the investigator to identify all the puzzle pieces and then put them together. In gathering puzzle pieces, you may find that not all the gathered pieces belong to this specific picture.

What if this is the third time an employee has filed a complaint against the same co-worker and the first two were closed as unsubstantiated? Does that mean the complainant is a liar and therefore never capable of telling the truth? Of course not. Like the young sheep herder, the third allegation may be true regardless of the veracity of the first two. Don't write off an allegation just because you don't want to deal with it. That is what the townsfolk did.

With the boy who cried wolf, the townsfolk had proven there was no threat on the first two nights because they responded to the call and investigated. The young herder also admitted that he had just wanted company and concocted the threat for excitement. In your case, you must look at why the first two were closed. Answering the "why" will often provide the context you need for your credibility assessment. Maybe there was positive proof that the previous allegations were false, just as with our sheep herder. But you must ask yourself:

- Were the first two investigations competent and thorough?

- Were they correctly documented?

- Did you conduct the investigations, or was it a coworker or the previous person in your position? Consider the possibility that you are a better investigator now than you were then and maybe missed something before. If it wasn't you, maybe the person who did the investigation wasn't trained like you are.

- Is it possible the allegations were actually true and there just was not sufficient evidence for a finding? It could be that the investigator conducted a very thorough investigation but there just wasn't enough evidence. This does not make the allegations false, just unsubstantiated. There is a big difference.

Maybe instead of being just another instance of "crying wolf," there will be enough evidence available in this third report to have a finding. It is also very possible that the third report will create enough evidence, when combined with the first two reports, to establish a pattern of misconduct or the existence of a persistent hostile work environment. A thorough investigation will bring the truth to light.

On the other hand, you must also consider the possibility that the allegations themselves are a form of harassment against the respondent. If the complainant is continually filing unsubstantiated complaints, then you may have a different form of misconduct and must deal with that independently. You should open a separate investigation into the allegation of false statements or false complaints. This eventuality should be written into your conduct policy. Take care, however, to ensure that you are differentiating between a false allegation and an unsubstantiated one. Just as you must have sufficient supporting evidence to have a finding of misconduct, you must have the same level of evidence to support a finding of making a false allegation.

I pose these questions and different possibilities to make a point. Each investigation must stand on its own and be worked thoroughly and independently. Basing your conclusion solely on past credibility or a past investigative conclusion is simple laziness. Laziness destroyed the townsfolk's sheep herd, and could destroy your career or your company.

I once had a case involving a minor male accused of sexual assault. When the investigation yielded insufficient evidence for a finding, a person reviewing the investigation asked why I did not use the male's behavior history in my analysis. The person asking me the question assumed that I might have found instances where the respondent was unruly in class, was a bully, or something else to that effect. The questioner spoke as if the respondent being disrespectful to a teacher in the past was somehow related to whether or not he sexually assaulted a girl in the present. The two were not related in any way, and I could not justly find that a young man committed sexual assault because he may have had a behavior problem. He was asking me to assess credibility based on completely unrelated behaviors and incidents.

I explained to my questioner that unless the past behavior included related or relevant behavior, that it was improper to include it in my assessment. Everyone has a history. Any use of past behavior must be directly linked to the current allegation. Could there have been a situation where past behavior was relevant? Of course. For example, if the respondent had a history of lying after being accused, that would have caused me to examine his current statement with that history in mind. Corroboration would have been key. Furthermore, if he had a history of using the same explanation or alibi as he did with me, that would be a relevant fact I would have investigated further. But as you can see, those behaviors would have been related and relevant. In this case, there was no relevant historical information, meaning I did not find it necessary to include any history in my assessment.

SECTION 5

STANDARD OF EVIDENCE

Prior to conducting any investigations, your organization needs to decide on the standard of evidence that will be used in all cases. This should be detailed in your conduct policy. I am not going to focus on the process of making that decision or using it to form your investigatory conclusion, but rather how the standard impacts your credibility assessment.

The most common standard of evidence used for administrative investigations is the preponderance of evidence (PoE) standard. This makes sense because it is also the standard used in civil courts, so if your investigation is ever challenged in court, the standards applied are consistent. It is important for you to understand what PoE means and how to judge credibility based on that standard.

In simple terms, PoE means more likely than not, or just over 50%. You should be asking yourself that question frequently throughout the investigation. "Is it more likely than not that this is true?" "Is it more likely than not that there is a wolf attacking the sheep?" But wait! Here's the kicker. Once you answer the yes/no question, you must again ask yourself *why*. You must be able to explain in writing why it is more likely than not. This forces you to go outside of your preconceived opinions, your gut feeling, or your biases. You must have evidence or information that backs up and supports your answer. If you can't explain the why, then you need to reassess and investigate further.

SECTION 6

HOW TO ASSESS CREDIBILITY - EVIDENCE BASED PRACTICES

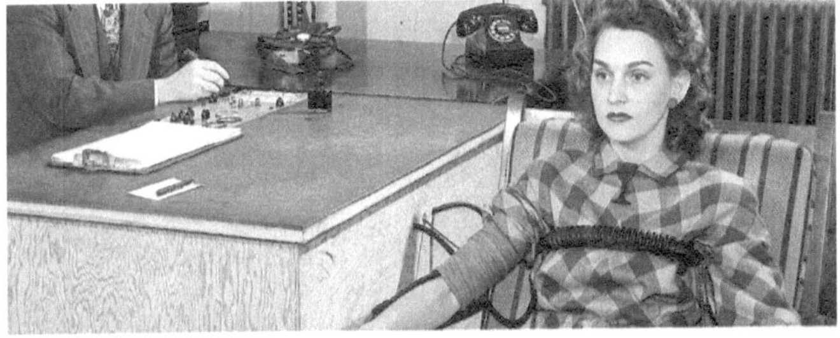

Credibility assessments must be based on more than just a gut feeling or emotional response. Despite what we see on television, human beings are actually horrible lie detectors. An experienced investigator may be better than the average citizen, but any honest investigator will be the first to admit there is no definitive way to know if someone is telling the truth. There is no magic body language dictionary. I recall a television show where a savant was able to discern if someone was lying just by observing their physical movements and reactions. His job was to help select juries using those skills. This was pure fiction.

Are there indicators of deception? Yes! Should you invest in training? Of course. This should be a part of any good interview training. But again, even after learning all of the possible indicators of deception and then factoring for culture, language, religion, background, education, environment, etc, those indicators are simply a guidepost, a starting point on the path to establishing the truth.

I once participated in a polygraph research project. Each participant was provided with instructions to either walk around campus for an hour or to steal a purse from a specified office, the purse having been planted there for the experiment. The polygrapher did not know which instruction I received. I was then hooked up to the polygraph machine and questioned to determine if I was the thief. They instructed everyone to say they did not steal the purse, even if they had. The polygrapher completed the exam and made his assessment prior to asking me which instruction I had received. He explained to me that he thought I had been lying and almost concluded that I had failed the test. However, his software, which was much more fine tuned, concluded I was telling the truth, which was correct. Even in this controlled environment, a polygrapher needed the help of complex software to determine if I was credible.

Take the inherent difficulty in determining if someone is lying and apply it to an emotionally charged situation. You will not be dealing with subjects in a controlled experiment. You will be speaking with emotionally involved human beings who are facing potentially devastating consequences. Your interviewees desperately want you to believe them. Think back to the five percent embellishment exercise.

You must always back up your assessment with evidence discovered through hard work and founded on training and experience. I learned this lesson the hard way. At a point in my career when I had years of experience under my belt and felt very confident, probably over confident, I had a sexual assault case where the complainant's story was not very credible. She seemed to have ulterior motives for making the report relating to her job performance rating. Quite simply, her story did not make sense. She accused the respondent of engaging in acts that did not seem reasonable. When she provided her statement, she showed common signs of deception.

On the other hand, the suspect provided a much more reasonable story. He was believable, sincere, and even agreed to take a polygraph without hesitation. His body language was open, and he did not show any signs of deception. I believed him and concluded in my mind he was innocent before the investigation was complete. Luckily, I continued to work the investigation to completion instead of stopping. But I thought I was just checking boxes leading to an inevitable closure. I scheduled the polygraph, and to my utter surprise, the polygraph showed deception. In the subsequent interview, he not only admitted he had lied in his initial statement to me, but confirmed the complainant's "far- fetched" story in detail. I learned a very important lesson about the limits of my ability to assess credibility, even after ten years of professional investigations experience.

This experience also reinforced the concept that it is very important not to make credibility assessments based on how you think a person should act. There is no set way a victim should or does act, nor is there a required reaction from a respondent. This applies both to the interview as well as during the incident itself. Everyone behaves and reacts in their own way based on their personality, experiences, background, and education. During a traumatic event, we often don't have any control over how we react. Our brain takes over in what is commonly referred to as the fight, flight, or freeze response.

I am unable to even count the number of times I have heard a witness say definitively that the alleged offense did not occur. When I explored how the witness knew with such certainty, expecting an eyewitness account or bombshell piece of evidence, I was always disappointed. The witnesses almost always said it was because that is not how a victim would act if she were truly assaulted. Often, the witness would cite a personal experience or an experience of another close friend or relative. The witness argued that because they reacted in a certain way previously, that the complainant was lying because she reacted differently this time. Logically, this makes no sense, but the witness was convinced and able to convince others. It is a persuasive, albeit fallacious, argument. If there existed a matrix defining how every person will react in every situation, we would never have to do the work required to get to the truth of a situation. We could be like the lazy townsfolk and simply refer to the chart. She didn't cry hard enough? Stamp the report *unsubstantiated*. Next!

As you obtain more training and experience in interviewing, you will learn to put aside your expectations of how a person should behave. You will learn to judge each individual independently by observing the totality of their behavior. Take note of any discrepancies or behaviors that are causing you concern and then analyze them as you continue your investigation. Often, you will find that there is a perfectly reasonable explanation for something that, at first, you thought was an indication of deception.

For example, in one of my sexual assault investigations, the victim's friend took a video of the victim immediately after the assault to show bruises that she obtained from her assailant. However, during the video, the victim laughed. I spoke with another investigator who dismissed the case because he said prosecutors could never win a case with a video of a laughing victim. He said no one would believe her, with the subtext being that he didn't believe her.

He was correct in one respect. Her behavior was not what people would see as normal or expected. It needed to be investigated further. Taking note of the behavior, when I spoke with the witness who took the video I asked her about it. I learned that the victim frequently laughed when she was upset or uncomfortable. It was a defense mechanism for her. As such, the videographer said she was actually trying to make the victim laugh to keep her from becoming upset. The witness explained that the victim was so traumatized that she needed help to jump into her normal defense mechanism of laughter. This testimony provided a very reasonable explanation for the behavior, and in my opinion, strengthened the case. That the victim normally used laughter as a defense mechanism became an easy point to corroborate. What at first seemed an insurmountable issue with the case ultimately wasn't even an issue.

On another occasion, I assumed a case from another investigator. He had essentially closed his case after his initial interview with the victim after making a half-hearted effort to have the victim engage in a pretext phone call with the suspect. He did not provide any training or coaching prior to the pretext call, and his report clearly showed he only did it to check the box. He felt she was not very believable and found issues with her statement. I picked up the case and, during the course of my investigation, found reasonable explanations for all of the supposed flaws in her statement. In reality, she had issues with her mental and physical health which impacted her ability to communicate. The original investigator never asked about her health nor made any attempt to explain why her statement looked as it did. I was able to develop a body of evidence that ended up supporting her statement. The incident had triggered a traumatic medical reaction, which logically addressed the issues the investigator had listed.

I began my case with no preconceived notions of credibility, but ultimately found her more credible because the evidence supported her statement. In addition to the medical evidence, I found text conversations supporting the allegations. Therein lies the key—credibility supported by evidence. The original investigator was not wrong in pointing out the issues with her original statement. His failure was in not following through to investigate the cause of those issues.

In one more example, I had three women who all made allegations against the same man. He denied any and all accusations. I could have assumed that the women had conspired together; that they thought three allegations would be more believable than one. I could have also taken the opposite extreme and just assumed guilt based on the fact that there were three allegations. Although there was no indication of conspiracy, I made no assumptions.

Instead of making assumptions, it became a part of my investigation to look into the relationship between the complainants. I was able to determine that not only did the three women not know each other, but that their reports were all made independently and without knowledge of the others. They never learned the names of the other complainants during the course of the investigation. I did this purposefully, which helped me establish and support the independent nature of their accounts. One of the complainants had actually come into the office months previously to ask questions about the investigative process, but declined at that time to provide the respondent's name or move forward. It was while I was in the midst of investigating the other two cases that she came in without warning and told me her assailant's name. After recovering from the shock of hearing the name of the man about whom I had received two other allegations, I was able to move forward with a third distinct, yet related, investigation.

By proving that each report was independent, the individual cases strengthened each other because of the similarities in the allegations. They showed a clear pattern of behavior. The respondent's denials were not credible because of the evidence against him, provided in three separate cases by three strangers. Furthermore, the complainants were each deemed credible based on both the evidence discovered in their own cases, as well as the nature of their cases in relation to one another.

In each of my examples, you can see that it would have been very easy for my investigations to be directed by an initial assessment. But, as a professional investigator, it is your responsibility to set those impressions aside and not make any assessments until you have all the relevant supporting evidence.

EXERCISE 3

Before continuing to the next section, conduct the following experiment. Choose a video online that depicts an incident of misconduct. It could be a car crash or a package being stolen from a front porch. It does not have to be something graphic. Now gather a group of co-workers or friends. When everyone is seated around the table but still distracted, talking to each other or looking at their phone, press play on the video without saying a word. When the video ends, explain that they each just witnessed a crime and ask them to pull out a piece of paper and describe everything that happened. You can continue the exercise by writing all of the responses on the board and discussing the incident, or you can take their answers back to look through on your own.

You will find that while everyone may agree that a package was stolen, there will be large discrepancies in the details. No two people will provide the same description of the thief, the getaway car, the porch, the yard, the time of day, or any other relevant details. As you begin to process these accounts, you will find patterns, but you will also learn that you cannot rely on any one statement. You conducted this exercise in a safe, controlled environment. Now add the element of trauma and imagine how that would impact memory and descriptions.

I recently responded to a fatal crash in front of my residence. I was not there in any official capacity, only as a resident. Professionally, I have received extensive training and practice in observing and documenting traumatic incidents. I provided my statement to the responding officers, confident in its accuracy. A few days later, I read an article online wherein the reporter interviewed my neighbor, who also responded. The article contained details that were simply not true. They didn't change the tragic nature of the accident and were not really significant, but caused me to review my own memories. I had to remind myself that humans do not make very good witnesses, especially when the experience in question is traumatic.

Even though I was not "on the job," I still responded as I was trained to do—as a professional, while my neighbor was simply experiencing the event. She was not a witness; she was a participant. This is an important distinction. As you are conducting your interview and assessing credibility, take note of the person's role in the incident. Are they describing something they witnessed, or something that happened to them?

WHAT DOES SUPPORTING EVIDENCE LOOK LIKE?

We have discussed the importance of an evidence-based credibility assessment, but what is considered evidence? If you are a law enforcement investigator, you are bound by strict rules of evidence. When conducting an administrative misconduct investigation, the rules are less stringent.

However, you should still maintain consistent evidence practices. Even though you do not have a secure evidence locker, you should still be able to articulate how and when you received the evidence, as well as how or where it was stored.

Evidence is information in any form. It can be written, narrative, graphic, video, or anything else. Remember, you are putting together a puzzle. Every piece of information is a piece of the puzzle. Your job is to determine if the piece is truly a part of your puzzle. You may develop some evidence on your own, but it is also important to ask the involved parties for evidence.

Ask them with the realization that they do not know what is relevant or important. They will either provide insufficient information and require some prodding, or they will provide every little thing they can think of. I recall a case involving two people who had been in a turbulent relationship. The allegation was that the man had assaulted the woman at specific points in the relationship. When I asked the complainant for evidence, she provided over 1000 pages of texts and emails to prove to me what a horrible person he was. To her, if she could prove he was a bad person, then it followed that he must have assaulted her. I reviewed every page and found maybe ten that were relevant to the allegations. Those ten were part of the puzzle.

As you are planning your investigation, try to think of what kind of evidence would corroborate the allegations. As you conduct each interview, think about all of the facts that you could possibly corroborate, and then identify what kind of evidence would properly do so. If your interviewee states that he emailed his boss about the discrepancy in accounts, ask for that email. Or even better, if you have the ability, ask your email administrator to pull that email out of the system. If your complainant said she couldn't stop crying after she was assaulted in the copy room, think of ways to corroborate that she was crying. Do you have cameras in the copy room, hallway, or office spaces? Are there any co-workers who saw her crying? Did she text a friend describing how upset she was? You are the investigator. Your job is to wade through the mountain of evidence and determine what is relevant and what is noise.

You must remember that the parties in the investigation do not know what is relevant or which details need specific corroboration. It is acceptable to ask for specific things, like an email or texts, but I would encourage you to also ask them generally to provide anything they believe is relevant. You may receive information that you didn't know existed.

Just as in the experience I related above, you may not be able to control how much information you receive. If you receive 1000 pages, it is your job to read every page. Do not make assumptions or be lazy in your review. The one nugget of information you need may be buried on page 893. You won't know unless you review everything.

It may appear that I am mixing evidence supporting the allegation and evidence supporting credibility. That is true, and I have done so on purpose. During the investigation, it is your job to collect all of the evidence, whether it serves one or both. It is only after collection that you will be able to analyze and evaluate the evidence.

As you are reviewing statements, ask yourself if there is evidence corroborating the facts. Ask yourself if there is evidence that explains discrepancies. We have already established that humans are fallible and witness testimony is problematic. Your job is to use the evidence to support the facts as much as possible. Refer to some of my examples. If you find the complainant has medical issues that impact her ability to express herself clearly, ask for medical documentation to corroborate her condition. If the complainant is laughing after the assault, obtain witness testimony regarding that reaction. If the respondent says he could not have done it because he has an alibi, follow up with an inquiry of that alibi. As you build a strong body of evidence, you will often see a pattern emerge where one person's story is more supported by the evidence. You are establishing credibility.

Remember, you will rarely have direct proof of misconduct. The puzzle rarely comes already put together in the box. When evaluating each piece of evidence, use your standard of proof. Ask yourself if your conclusion is more likely than not what happened.

Your company does not expect you to prove the allegation beyond a reasonable doubt, and you will rarely be able to do so without having law enforcement-type authority. But it is very possible to meet or exceed the PoE standard if you are thorough and put in the work.

SECTION 8

WHAT WEIGHT SHOULD YOUR ASSESSMENT CARRY?

Your primary goal in conducting the investigation and putting together your puzzle is to determine if the allegation is supported up to the PoE standard. Do not get caught in the trap of thinking your job is to determine guilt or innocence. In fact, you should never allow yourself or your team to use the word innocent, even if it applies to the situation, because that is not your role. Your job is not to prove a negative. You are investigating whether or not the allegations are supported to the PoE standard. Period. Again, referring to the criminal justice system, juries do not find defendants guilty or innocent. Defendants are either found guilty or not guilty. Not guilty is very different than innocent.

Credibility should be as small a factor in your conclusion as possible. People often refer to difficult sexual assault cases as "he said - she said" cases. People rarely engage in intimate behavior in front of witnesses; therefore, it is commonly thought the case is his word against hers. As an investigator, you know this is not true. There is always evidence. It is your job to know where to look, what to look for, and what information is relevant. The more evidence you can gather and the further away you can get from a dueling statements scenario, the more solid and informed your conclusion will be.

If you find yourself weighing credibility too heavily, you will see that you are allowing your biases and expectations to infiltrate the investigation. The evidence that supports credibility will often also support the allegations, and should be used as the latter.

If you have an investigation where evidence is limited and credibility becomes a large factor, be careful that you are basing your assessment on evidence that is relevant and related. Do not force a finding solely on your credibility assessment. If the evidence is not there, it is not there, and you must conclude that the allegations were not supported, even if you personally believe them to be true. Remember the case where I was asked to look at the teenage boy's behavior? He was a teenage boy. I am sure I could have searched until I found instances of bad behavior. No one is perfect. I could have forced that puzzle piece into my puzzle. But that would have been neither professional nor fair.

If you have a large body of evidence proving that one of the parties is not credible, don't be afraid to use it. I once had a case where the respondent was giving different facts in a concurrent but separate investigation regarding the same allegations, and he changed his story whenever confronted about the differences. I had a large body of evidence showing that he was not credible. In that case, credibility did weigh heavily, but it was because he told lies directly related to the case. There are multiple scenarios where concurrent investigations exist, most frequently in criminal and administrative cases.

A good practice is to weigh the evidence supporting the allegation first. If you have a finding based on that evidence, there is no need to formally assess credibility. But if your interpretation of the evidence requires a credibility assessment, be sure to articulate very clearly how the evidence is relevant.

SECTION 9

PITFALLS AND LIMITATIONS OF CREDIBILITY ASSESSMENTS

We have already discussed how, despite your best intentions, you do not make a very good lie detector. Although you will become better with time and expe- rience, credibility assessments are rarely definitive. Humans operate on the spectrum between absolute truth and absolute falsehood.

If you conscientiously work every aspect of the investigation and avoid making premature conclusions, you will be able to avoid the pitfalls of false credibility. One of the most frequent mistakes is judging credibility based on presentation or appearance. We have all been taught since childhood to avoid judging a book by its cover, yet we all do just that every day. I have frequently heard people say that a person could not have committed a crime because they are such a good employee, they volunteer in the community, they go to church, or they do other so called good things. One of the most common defenses I have heard when interviewing rape suspects is that they could have never done such a thing because they have sisters, or their mom taught them to respect women. This carries no relevance.

Do not allow yourself to start considering information that is not relevant just because you personally feel a certain way. It would be very easy to agree with that defense, because how could a person with sisters do such a thing? You must put those thoughts aside, even if they make sense to you. Do not fall victim to confirmation bias.

I have seen examples of investigators who believed one party over the other because one was dressed more professionally. I have seen examples of investigators believing the party who had the resources to hire an attorney over the one who did not. We already discussed the danger of judging someone based on your expectations of how they should act.

There are two ways to avoid common pitfalls:

1. Assess credibility supported by evidence.

2. Assess statements from the subject's perspective, not your own.

We have already discussed the first rule at length, so I will focus here on the second. We naturally assess every situation through our own lens. It is very difficult to see from another person's perspective or to step into their shoes. But this is imperative. You are not assessing whether the alleged event happened to you, so your perspective is not what is important to the case. If you believe a complainant acted in an illogical way, place yourself in his shoes, using his statement and explanation. Given his experience, personality, values, etc., is his reaction reasonable? Maybe this is the second time he has reported being a victim and the first time no one believed him. Is it reasonable that he was afraid the same thing would happen again? My victim in the bad relationship felt very strongly that she had to prove fully that her boyfriend was a bad person in order for me to believe her. Is it reasonable that she herself did not quite understand the psychological reasons why she kept going back to such an abusive boyfriend and therefore thought I would also judge her? If you find yourself having difficulty understanding from their perspective, do some research, pursue training on the subject, or ask an expert.

You do not have to have gone through the same experience that you are investigating in order to see it from their perspective. As an investigator, you need to work on that skill. It requires deliberate action and practice. But over time, you will be able to step outside of your own experiences to view your investigation from different perspectives.

Conclusion

Assessing credibility is imperative, but do not use it as a short-cut or crutch. You have to complete every step of the investigation. Assess credibility based on the evidence you gather, not on feelings or hunches. Do not allow your like or dislike of one of the parties to influence your decision. You are not a lie detector and never will be. Do not lose your entire herd of sheep simply because you believe X+Y=Z. X, Y, and Z are all unique incidents that stand on their own. If you find one party more credible, you should be able to articulate why with information that is relevant and connected to the investigation. Do not fall into the trap of basing your findings solely on past incidents or old information.

If you cannot explain your reasoning in writing, then you are not ready to make your assessment. Return, reassess, reevaluate.

Learning to judge what evidence or information is relevant to your case may seem a daunting task. It comes with training and experience. If you want to avoid losing your entire herd of sheep, but are unsure of how to move forward, find help from experienced, quality investigators. As you focus on obtaining and corroborating evidence, you will begin to understand how they relate to your credibility assessment.

Author's Note

Throughout this book I may have used some terms interchangeably. Each use is acceptable and you may use different language in your policy. For example:

Victim - Complainant

Suspect - Respondent - Assailant - Accused

Allegation - Accusation

I have also used different gender pronouns throughout the book to facilitate the ease of reading. Misconduct allegations can be made by or against any gender and no meaning is attached to my use of specific pronouns throughout the book.

ACKNOWLEDGMENTS

Editing and design by Lena Dalley of Dal-eLearning, LLC

Design by David Dalley of Dal-eLearning, LLC

Editing by Caleb Williams of Caleb Williams Editing and Illustration

Attributions

OTHER BOOKS IN THE SERIES

Find additional training and resources in the following books:

Convincing Leadership

Tips for Leaders in Preparing for Misconduct

Bias in Investigations

The Impact of Screwing Up

MARCUS WILLIAMS TRAINING ACADEMY